# Jimmy Carter

Published in the United States of America by Cherry Lake Publishing
Ann Arbor, Michigan
www.cherrylakepublishing.com

Content Adviser: Ryan Emery Hughes, Doctoral Student, School of Education, University of Michigan
Reading Adviser: Marla Conn, ReadAbility, Inc.
Book Design: Jennifer Wahi
Illustrator: Jeff Bane

Photo Credits: © Jeffrey M. Frank/Shutterstock Images, 5; © Carter Family Photographs/National Archives
and Records Association, 7; © Courtesy: Jimmy Carter Presidential Library, 9, 15, 17, 22, 23; © Joe Gough/
Shutterstock Images, 11; © ZUMA Press, Inc. / Alamy Stock Photo, 13; © EdStock/istockphoto.com, 19;
© Nir Levy/Shutterstock Images, 21; Cover, 6, 10, 18, Jeff Bane; Various frames throughout, Shutterstock Images

Library of Congress Cataloging-in-Publication Data

Haldy, Emma E.
  Jimmy Carter / by Emma E. Haldy ; illustrated by Jeff Bane.
    pages cm --  (My itty-bitty bio)
  Includes bibliographical references and index.
  ISBN 978-1-63471-014-5 (hardcover) -- ISBN 978-1-63471-015-2 (pdf) -- ISBN 978-1-63471-016-9 (pbk.) -- ISBN
978-1-63471-017-6 (ebook)
  1.  Carter, Jimmy, 1924---Juvenile literature. 2.  Presidents--United States--Biography--Juvenile literature.  I. Bane,
Jeff, 1957- illustrator. II. Title.

E873.H35 2016
973.926092--dc23
  [B]

                                        2015034566

Printed in the United States of America
Corporate Graphics

# table of contents

**About the author:** Emma E. Haldy is a former librarian and a proud Michigander. She lives with her husband, Joe, and an ever-growing collection of books.

**About the illustrator:** Jeff Bane and his two business partners own a studio along the American River in Folsom, California, home of the 1849 Gold Rush. When Jeff's not sketching or illustrating for clients, he's either swimming or kayaking in the river to relax.

I was born in Georgia. It was 1924.

My father was a peanut farmer. He also ran a store. My mother was a nurse.

What job would you want?

I enjoyed reading.
I liked fishing.

I was good at school.
I graduated from the
U.S. Naval Academy.

I fell in love with Rosalynn Smith.
We got married.

We had four children.

I served in the Navy. I worked on a submarine.

When my father died, I went home. I took over his peanut farm.

I wanted to help my community.
I became a **politician**.

I was **elected** governor of Georgia.

How would you like to help
your community?

I thought I could make America better. I was elected president.

I helped the **environment**.
I worked on world peace and **human rights**.

But my job was not easy. There were problems I could not fix. I lost the next election.

I moved back to Georgia. I have been here ever since. My work goes on.

I still talk to troubled countries.
I help them find peace.

I love to help the
poor. I build houses
for those in need.

Nobel PEACE PRIZE

I write books. I give speeches. I inspire others to follow my example.

I am proud that I have helped people across the globe. I have made the world a better place.

What would you like to ask me?

**1946**

**1920**

**Born
1924**

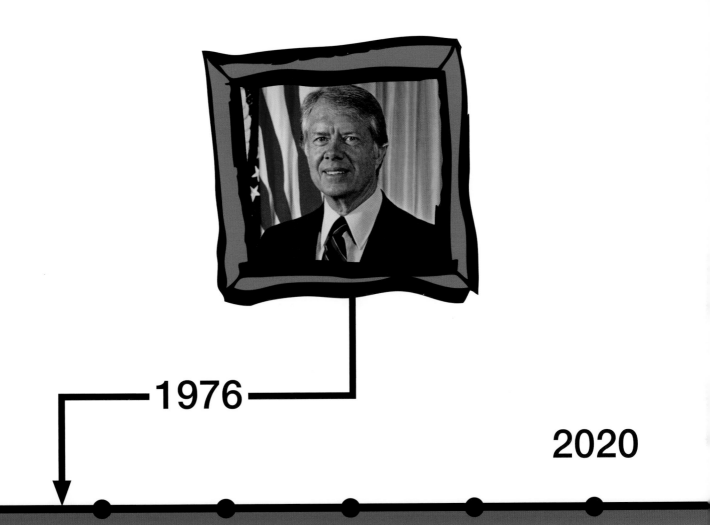

1976

2020

## glossary

**elected** (i-LEKT-id) chosen by people who voted

**environment** (en-VYE-ruhn-muhnt) the natural surroundings of living things, such as the air, land, or sea

**human rights** (HYOO-muhn RITES) rights that all people are entitled to hold, like freedom and equality

**politician** (pah-li-TISH-uhn) a person elected to the government

## index